ANCIENT AND MEDIEVAL PEOPLE

The Spartan Hoplites

Louise Park
and Timothy Love

Marshall Cavendish
Benchmark
New York

This edition first published in 2010 in the United States of America by Marshall Cavendish Benchmark.

Marshall Cavendish Benchmark
99 White Plains Road
Tarrytown, NY 10591
www.marshallcavendish.us

All Internet sites were available and accurate when sent to press.

First published in 2009 by
MACMILLAN EDUCATION AUSTRALIA PTY LTD
15–19 Claremont Street, South Yarra 3141

Visit our website at www.macmillan.com.au or go directly to www.macmillanlibrary.com.au

Associated companies and representatives throughout the world.

Library of Congress Cataloging-in-Publication Data

Park, Louise, 1961–
    The Spartan hoplites / by Louise Park and Timothy Love.
        p. cm. – (Ancient and medieval people)
    ISBN 978-0-7614-4449-7
    1. Sparta (Extinct city)–History, Military–Juvenile literature. 2. Soldiers–Greece–Sparta (Extinct city)–Juvenile literature. 3. Greece–History–Persian Wars, 500-449 B.C.–Campaigns–Juvenile literature. I. Love, Timothy. II. Title.
    DF261.S8P37 2009
    938'.9–dc22

                            2008055779

Edited by Julia Carlomagno
Text and cover design by Cristina Neri, Canary Graphic Design
Page layout by Cristina Neri, Canary Graphic Design
Photo research by Legend Images
Illustrations by Colby Heppéll, Giovanni Caselli, and Paul Konye

Printed in the United States

Acknowledgments
The author and the publisher are grateful to the following for permission to reproduce copyright material:

Front cover photos: Ancient acropolis at Corinth, Greece © Styve Reineck/Shutterstock; parchment © Selahattin BAYRAM/iStockphoto

Photos courtesy of: Background photos throughout: old paper © peter zelei/iStockphoto; mosaic tiles © Hedda Gjerpen/iStockphoto; Corinthian column © PhotographerOlympus/iStockphoto; Coo-ee Historical Picture Library, **28**; Giovanni Caselli's Universal Library Unlimited, **6, 9, 14, 21, 22, 23, 24, 25, 29, 30**; Hulton Archive/Getty Images, **18, 19**; Mansell/Time Life Pictures/Getty Images, **15**; Hulton Archive/Getty Images via iStockphoto, **20**; Photolibrary © Ivy Close Images/Alamy, **16**; Photolibrary © North Wind Picture Archives/Alamy, **17, 27**; Photolibrary/Mary Evans Picture Library, **26**; Wikimedia Commons, photo by Johnny Shumate, **12**.

Sources for quotes used in text: Quote from he historian Myron cited in *Sparta and Lakonia*, p. 354, **8**; Adapted quote from the historian Plutarch in *On Sparta*, pp. 40–1, **8**.

The authors and publisher wish to advise that to the best of their ability they have tried to verify dates, facts, and the spelling of personal names and terminology. The accuracy and reliability of some information on ancient civilizations is difficult in instances where detailed records were not kept or did not survive.

1 3 5 6 4 2

Contents

Glossary Words

When a word is printed in **bold**, you can look up its meaning in the Glossary on page 31.

Who Were the Spartan Hoplites?

The Spartan hoplites were trained soldiers who served in the Spartan army. They were skilled fighters who **conquered** many areas around Sparta.

Ancient Sparta

Ancient Sparta was a Greek **city-state** located near Athens. It was known for its powerful army. Sparta was formed around 950 BCE, when four local tribes joined together to conquer the land of Laconia. The city-state of Sparta was built on the banks of the Eurotas River, in the valley beneath Mount Taygetos.

Ancient Sparta Timeline

480 BCE
Sparta becomes involved in the Persian Wars

457 BCE
Sparta is at war with Athens

464 BCE
The slaves **revolt**

480 BCE   460 BCE   440 BCE   42

The ancient city-state of Sparta was located near Athens, in Greece.

Key
The Spartan Empire
Scale
600 miles
100 kilometers

The Development of the Spartan Army

The Spartan army developed as Sparta grew in strength and size. When Sparta was first established, the conquered Laconian people became either helots or periokoi. Helots were slaves, while periokoi were merchants and traders. Male members of the tribes that conquered Laconia became Spartiate **citizens**. As Sparta grew, these Spartiate citizens formed a government and the Spartan army. For hundreds of years, all Spartiate citizens fought in the Spartan army.

WHAT'S IN A NAME?
Hoplite
The word *hoplite* comes from the Greek word *hoplon*. A hoplon was the type of shield carried by soldiers. The word *periokoi* is also Greek and means "dwellers around."

404 BCE
Sparta defeats Athens

400 BCE

380 BCE

360 BCE

412 BCE
Sparta forms an alliance with Persia

371 BCE
Sparta loses to the Thebans at the Battle of Leuktra

Spartan Society

Spartan society was made up of several **social classes**, including the Spartiate citizens, the periokoi, and the helots. The periokoi and the helots were dominated by the Spartiate citizens.

Spartiate Citizens

Spartiate citizens were men who had completed the Spartan training system known as the Agoge. Spartan women were not considered strong enough to fight. If they did not complete this training system, they were labeled **outcasts** and made to wear different clothing as a form of **public humiliation**.

Originally, Spartiate citizens were the only people allowed to become hoplite soldiers. The hoplites had a strong code of honor and they sought glory in battle and in death. It has been noted that Spartan women would say to their husbands in times of war, "come home with your shield, or come home on it."

Only men could become Spartiate citizens. As citizens, they were expected to fight in the Spartan army.

The Periokoi

The periokoi were the free people of the lands of Messenia and Lakonia. They were the traders, merchants, and fishers of Sparta. Some historians have noted that they also made shoes, clothing, and tools. The periokoi sometimes had the right to a trial if accused of committing a crime, although the Spartan government could sentence them to death without trial, too.

Quick Facts

What Were the Benefits of Being a Spartiate Citizen?

People who became Spartiate citizens did not have to work and were given land.

❖ Spartiate citizens were wealthy. Their wealth came from land and property worked on by helots.

❖ Spartiate citizens were banned from trade or manufacturing work. This work was done by the periokoi.

❖ At the beginning of the 500s BCE it is thought that there were around ten thousand Spartiate citizens. By 244 BCE there were fewer than seven hundred citizens left.

Members of the periokoi made weapons and armor for the Spartan hoplites.

7

The Helots

The helots were slaves and peasants from the conquered lands of Messenia and Lakonia. They were owned by the city-state of Sparta, and they worked the land owned by Spartiate citizens. Helots were required to hand over half of their produce to their master. They had no legal or political rights.

Spartiate citizens believed they were **superior** to the helots and treated them cruelly. In 464 BCE, the helots revolted against the Spartiate citizens on Mount Ithome. The revolt was so powerful that the Spartans had to seek help from other Greek city-states in order to crush it.

Helots were slaves and workers in Sparta.

*They assign to the helots every shameful task leading to disgrace. For they **ordained** that each one of them must wear a dogskin cap and wrap himself in sins and receive a **stipulated** number of beatings every year regardless of any wrongdoing, so that they would never forget that they were slaves.*

—THE HISTORIAN MYRON

The Krypteia

The krypteia were thought to be Sparta's secret police, and they controlled the helots. Members of the krypteia targeted helots who stood out because of their fitness and strength, were leaders among other helots, or were outspoken about the Spartan government's policies. The krypteia captured and murdered these helots at night.

Many historians believe that serving in the krypteia was a rite of passage for Spartiate citizens, in order to complete the Agoge training. This would have taught the soldiers **stealth** and given them experience in hand-to-hand combat.

Krypteia would spy on helot homes at night, looking for signs of suspicious activities.

By day they would hide and rest. At night they would travel along roads and murder any helot that they caught… The historian Thucydides tells how over 2,000 helots were singled out by the Spartiates for their bravery, but then a little later they vanished, and nobody was able to explain how.

—ADAPTED FROM THE HISTORIAN PLUTARCH

Social Class in the Spartan Army

Social class played a large role in the formation and running of the Spartan army. It is believed that the Spartan army was formed partly to control helot revolts and **uprisings**. However, over time both helots and periokoi were allowed to serve in the army.

The Role of the Helots in the Spartan Army

Spartiate citizens had a great deal of pride in Sparta and, because of this, helots were not originally allowed to serve in the Spartan army. However, helots held a large amount of power because they made up the majority of Spartan society. Over time, helots were allowed to serve in the army, but they were never allowed to train in the Agoge.

In the later years of Spartan society, helots could fight alongside Spartiate citizens in the army.

The Role of the Periokoi in the Spartan Army

The periokoi were expected to fight as hoplites in the Spartan army during times of war. Like the helots, the periokoi did not train for the Agoge. Until around 465 BCE the periokoi and the Spartans fought separately, but records from the historian Herodotus indicate that they fought together after this time.

From the beginning of Spartan society, periokoi were expected to fight alongside Spartiate citizens in battles.

Spartan Weapons, Armor, and Warfare

T he Spartans were the dominant force in the **Aegean** for 400 years. Their success was partly due to their weapons, armor, and battle tactics.

Weapons and Armor

A Spartan hoplite carried a concave shield known as a hoplon. This shield was believed to be large enough to cover a hoplite's body from his thighs to his shoulders. He also carried a ten-foot-long (three-meter-long) spear, used for thrusting, and an iron sword.

A Spartan hoplite wore **distinctive** armor. He wore a bronze breastplate over a cloth tunic, and a thin bronze helmet. This helmet was often decorated with a crest of horsehair. The well-known Spartan **lawgiver** Lykurgus also made each hoplite wear a crimson cloak, believing that this made them look less like women. Hoplites under age thirty had short hair, while older hoplites could choose to grow their hair. All hoplites wore sandals.

Bronze helmet

Hoplon

Spear

Bronze breastplate

Iron sword

Cloth tunic

Sandals

Warfare

Spartan warfare was marked by the group strength and discipline that Spartan hoplites showed. The hoplites fought as a group, which was known as a **phalanx**.

An enōmotia division was made up of four groups of eight men. Today, it is known as a platoon.

A pentēkostys division was made up of four enōmatiai. Today, it is known as a company.

A lochos division was made up of two pentēkostyses. Today, it is known as a battalion.

A mora division was made up of four lochoi. Today, it is known as a regiment.

There were four different divisions in a Spartan phalanx.

Battle Formations

The hoplites had many bold battle formations. In one formation, each hoplite would cover the right side of his body with his shield. The left side was covered by the shield of the hoplite standing next to him. With their shields locked together, the hoplites advanced on enemies as a group, forming a moving bronze wall that was difficult for enemies to penetrate. This formation was used successfully in the Battle of Plataea, during the Persian Wars.

SPOTLIGHT ON
the Persian Wars

Spotlight On

WHAT: The Persian Wars

BETWEEN: The Persians and the Greeks

BEGAN: Around 499 BCE

ENDED: Around 448 BCE

The Persian Wars were fought between the Persians and the Greeks. The Greek city-states of Athens and Sparta were invaded by the Persian Empire on several occasions, and the wars that followed these invasions were defining moments in Sparta's history. Due to the strength of the Spartans and the Athenians, the Persian army never managed to conquer Greece.

Why Did the Persian Wars Occur?

The Persian Wars broke out because Sparta and Athens did not want to be controlled by Persia. Historians report that the Persians wanted the Greeks to serve in the Persian army and to pay extremely high taxes. The Greek city-states fought against the Persian invaders to maintain their independence from Persia.

Greek soldiers fought many bloody battles against the Persian invaders during the Persian Wars.

Persian Wars Timeline

500 BCE	495 BCE	490 BCE

500–499 BCE
Conflicts between the Greeks and the Persians

490 BCE
The Battle of Marathon

Battles During the Persian Wars

Many battles were fought between the Greeks and the Persians during the Persian Wars.

❖ The Battle of Marathon was fought between the Athenian army and the Persian army. The Spartans were unwilling to help the Athenians. With an army one-third the size of the Persian army, the Athenians defeated the Persians.

❖ The Battle of Thermopylae was fought by an alliance of Greek city-states. Although they were vastly outnumbered, the Spartan hoplites held off the Persian enemy for three days.

❖ The Battle of Salamis was a **naval** battle fought between the Greek city-states and Persia. It took place in the waters between Piraeus and Salamis. The victory of the Greek city-states in this battle is considered to be the turning point that led to the final Persian defeat.

❖ The Battle of Plataea was fought between Sparta and Persia on the slopes of Mount Cithaeron. The Spartan army, made up of hoplites and helots, defeated the Persian army. This battle marks Persia's last attempt to invade Greece.

The Battle of Marathon involved the Athenian army and the Persian army.

485 BCE   **480 BCE**   **475 BCE**

480 BCE
The Battle of Thermopylae and the Battle of Salamis

479 BCE
The Battle of Plataea

the Battle of Thermopylae

The Battle of Thermopylae is one of the most famous battles in Spartan history. There were said to be one thousand Persian soldiers for every Spartan hoplite present.

Thermopylae was a narrow road that cut through the mountains. It was the only way that the Persian army could get to Athens. During the battle, the Spartan army was betrayed and lost to the Persians after three days of fighting.

WHAT'S IN A NAME?

The Immortals

The Immortals earned their name because every time one soldier would die, he was immediately replaced with another soldier. Therefore, the group remained at full strength.

The First Days of Battle

The Spartans were very successful during the first days of the battle. On the first day, they formed a phalanx near their camp behind the Phocian Wall. The historian Ctestias noted that the first waves of Persian troops to attack the camp were "cut to pieces," while only two or three hoplites were killed. King Xerxes of Persia was angered by the Spartans' strength. He sent in his personal bodyguards and soldiers, known as the Immortals. These soldiers were also killed by the Spartans and their allies.

King Leonidas I was killed by Persian soldiers during the Battle of Thermopylae.

The Turning Point

The turning point in the battle came when a man from a nearby Greek city-state gave King Xerxes information in the hope of a great reward. He told King Xerxes about a mountain trail that led over the hills and into the Spartan camp. If the Persian army used this trail, they could surprise the Spartan hoplites and attack them from behind. King Xerxes marched troops over the trail and surrounded the Spartan soldiers. King Leonidas I, who was leading the Spartan army, managed to send away most of his troops. Only about three hundred soldiers were left to defend the pass, and they fought to the death.

What You Should Know About...

The Battle of Thermopylae

❖ The Spartan army blocked the pass long enough to keep the Persian army occupied while the rest of the Greek soldiers escaped.

❖ It is believed that King Leonidas I sent most of his troops away so that they could prepare for the Battle of Salamis.

❖ The three hundred Spartan hoplites who died defending the pass came to **embody** the Spartan ideal. They were seen as great examples of courage and self-sacrifice.

Three hundred Spartan soldiers defended the pass at Thermopylae.

Sparta's Government

The Spartan Government consisted of two kings, five ephors, the Gerousia, and the Apella. The Gerousia was a council that had the power to try citizens in court, including the king, and the Apella represented Spartan **democracy**.

Spartan Kings

Sparta had two kings, and both led the Spartan army. The kings were chosen from two royal families, the Agiads and the Eurypondids. According to Spartan legend, these families were descended from Hercules, the greatest of the Greek heroes.

Sparta was one of few Greek city-states that was a **monarchy**, rather than a democracy. A Spartan king was expected to fill the roles of chief priest, commander-in-chief of the army, judge, and lawgiver. The king always fought in battles. He led the soldiers into combat and was the last to leave the battlefield.

Sparta's kings could make laws to punish those who had committed a crime.

Spartan Ephors

The ephors were the kings' advisors and **war tacticians**, as well as the chief administrators and executors of Sparta. They welcomed visiting **ambassadors** and were in charge of the Agoge, and they could banish foreigners from Sparta. The ephors also had the power to imprison a king. This was a **safeguard** against **tyranny**. There were five ephors, one from each region of Sparta. They were elected annually and no man could serve in the role more than once. The ephors met daily to discuss issues.

The Gerousia

The Gerousia was a council of thirty-eight men over the age of sixty, as well as Sparta's two kings. This council served as Sparta's **aristocracy**. Although in theory any man could be elected to the Gerousia, in practice membership was very exclusive. Men from wealthy families were selected. The Gerousia prepared the business and agenda for the Apella. They could apply penalties of death, loss of citizenship, and exile, and were the only council allowed to try cases involving kings.

The Apella

The Apella was a council of Spartiate citizens who were thirty or older, and they met monthly. The Apella elected the ephors and the Gerousia, passed laws, decided on matters of war and peace, and resolved disputes. The Apella voted by **acclamation** and could only vote "yes" or "no."

King Cleombrotus was advised by the ephors when he faced difficult decisions about Sparta and its army.

IN PROFILE: King Leonidas I

In Profile

NAME: King Leonidas I

ALSO KNOWN AS: King of Sparta

BORN: 521 BCE

DIED: 480 BCE

King Leonidas I most likely came to power around 488 BCE. He was the son of Anaxandridas II, who ruled Sparta between 560 and 525 BCE. King Leonidas I is remembered for his bravery when leading the Spartan army at the Battle of Thermopylae in 480 BCE.

Notable Moment

During the Battle of Thermopylae, King Leonidas I and the Spartan army put up a brave fight against the Persians. A small force of Greek soldiers blocked the only road through Thermopylae, and the Spartan army's role was to protect this narrow pass. It is believed that the Persian army outnumbered the Spartan army by more than 100 to 1. Despite this, King Leonidas I's men held back the Persian army for three days.

King Leonidas I Timeline

520 BCE — **510 BCE** — **500 BCE**

521 BCE
Born in Sparta

Betrayed to the Persians

The Spartan army was betrayed by a local man called Ephialtes, who told the Persians of a secret mountain pass that led behind the Spartan army. When King Leonidas I found out about this betrayal, he dismissed most of his army and stayed behind to fight with three hundred Spartan hoplites. The Persians eventually killed King Leonidas I and his soldiers, then took the mountain path. However, they suffered a large number of **casualties** at the hands of the hoplites.

What You Should Know About...

King Leonidas I and Thermopylae

❖ King Leonidas I only chose fathers to fight at Thermopylae. If they were killed, their sons could carry on the family name.

❖ After King Leonidas I was killed, the Spartan soldiers protected his body until they were killed.

❖ Historians have debated whether the king's final actions were heroic or foolish. The historian Herodotus suggested that the Battle of Thermopylae gave the armies that were sent home time to prepare for the Battle of Salamis.

This statue of King Leonidas I stands in Sparta today.

490 BCE | 480 BCE | 470 BCE

488 BCE
Becomes king of Sparta

480 BCE
Dies in the Battle of Thermopylae

Training to Be a Spartan Hoplite

The training system for Spartan hoplites was known as the Agoge. Training for the Agoge began at the age of seven and was not completed until the age of thirty. Only boys were allowed to train for the Agoge.

Before the Agoge

The ephors inspected each boy born in Sparta ten days after his birth, to decide if he was fit to enter the Agoge. Any baby with **deformities** was thrown over the Apothetae, a cliff on Mount Taygetos. Those found free of deformities were allowed to join the Agoge.

Until the age of seven, boys were cared for by their mothers. Mothers were expected to teach their sons discipline and obedience in preparation for the Agoge.

The ephors inspected each boy born in Sparta to ensure that he did not have any deformities.

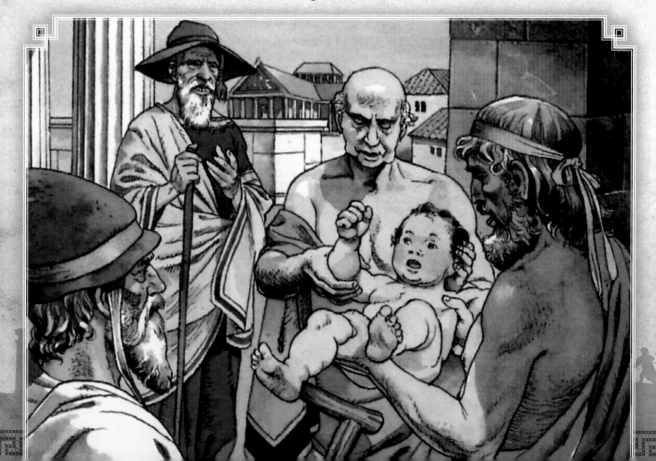

Spartan boys lived in military barracks and trained
in a central courtyard called a dromos.

Early Years of Training

At age seven, boys left their families and
moved to a barracks, which is a type of
military housing. Boys lived in groups,
which encouraged **camaraderie**. They
learned basic military skills, how to read
and write, and how to show obedience and
responsibility. At age ten, they began to
learn music, dancing, and athletics. These
activities taught them to be disciplined.

WHAT'S IN A NAME?

The Running of the Cheese

In the early years of training, Spartan
boys often played a game called the
running of the cheese. In this game, boys
stole cheese from monks and brought
it back to their barracks. The aim was
not to get caught. Spartan hoplites
were encouraged to learn how to steal
because they may have needed these
skills to survive in times of war.

Middle Years of Training

From the ages of twelve to eighteen, Spartan boys gained more responsibility. At twelve, boys exercised, slept on beds of **reeds**, and learned games that taught them endurance. They were fed **rations** and taught basic survival skills. They only wore one item of clothing and no shoes. At age eighteen, the boys were given the title of *eiren*. This allowed them to marry and serve in the Spartan army. However, they were not able to serve in the **front line** and those who chose to marry were not allowed to live with their wives until they had completed the Agoge training. Those with the title of eiren also held leadership roles over the younger boys in the Agoge.

When a Spartan boy was eighteen, he could serve in the Spartan army.

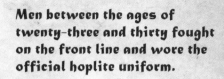

Men between the ages of twenty-three and thirty fought on the front line and wore the official hoplite uniform.

Late Years of Training

From the ages of twenty to thirty, Spartan men became hoplites. At age twenty men joined clubs known as *syssitia*, in which groups of soldiers ate together and bonded. Between the ages of twenty-three and twenty-nine, men became full-time soldiers in the Spartan army. At age thirty, men became Spartiate citizens and official hoplite soldiers. They were able to live at home and grow their hair.

Upon completing the Agoge training, groups of men were sometimes sent into the countryside, where they were forced to survive on their skill and strength. This was thought to be an **initiation** exercise. After this exercise, soldiers were passed into active reserve until the age of sixty. This meant they could be called upon to fight when needed.

Quick Facts

Did Spartan Females Receive Any Training?

Spartan females were not allowed to take part in the Agoge training but they received education and physical training.

❖ Spartan girls were raised by their mothers, who taught them reading, writing, dancing, and gymnastics.

❖ Women in Sparta were expected to remain at their physical peak. The Spartans believed that fit parents made healthy children.

SPOTLIGHT ON
the Battle of Plataea

Many Spartans were killed during the Battle of Plataea.

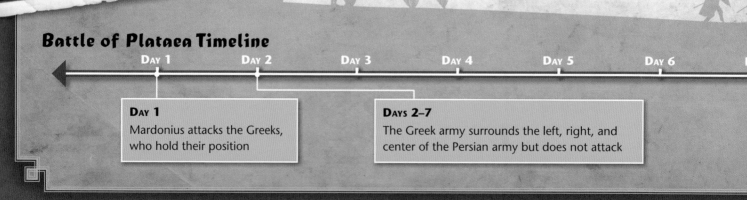

The Battle of Plataea was the first successful Greek **offensive** during the Persian Wars. It led to the end of the Persian Wars.

Origins of the Battle

After the Battle of Salamis, King Xerxes returned to Persia and left his military general, Mardonius, to fight the Greeks. Mardonius captured Athens and burned it to the ground. He then prepared to invade the nearby city of Plataea. The Plataeans asked the Spartan army for help and were sent the greatest force of Spartan soldiers ever seen in battle. The historian Herodotus noted that there were five thousand hoplite soldiers, five thousand periokoi, and 35,000 helots. All were under the command of Pausanias, the leader of the Spartan army.

The Persian Attack

After destroying Athens, Mardonius retreated to the city of Thebes, hoping to draw the Greeks into battle at nearby Plataea. He built a wooden **palisade** and positioned himself along the Asopus river near Plataea. The Greeks took position in the foothills of Mount Cithaeron, where the Persians attacked them repeatedly.

Battle of Plataea Timeline

DAY 1 DAY 2 DAY 3 DAY 4 DAY 5 DAY 6 D

DAY 1
Mardonius attacks the Greeks, who hold their position

DAYS 2–7
The Greek army surrounds the left, right, and center of the Persian army but does not attack

The Turning Point

Pausanias secretly moved his men down the foothills across the Asopus ridge. There they had access to fresh water in the Asopus spring and increased mobility. Mardonius ordered the poisoning of the Asopus spring, and soon after that the Greeks had no fresh water. Most Greek soldiers moved to a location closer to Plataea. The Spartans, however, moved to the Cithaeron Hills, which was closer to the Persian army. The Persians' line of sight was blocked by the hills, and they only saw the other Greeks moving away. They rushed forward to attack, and ran into the Spartan army.

Outcome of the Battle

The Spartans won the battle because their weapons and skills were superior to the Persians'. They fought with vigor to avenge the death of King Leonidas I, who was killed at the Battle of Thermopylae. During the battle, Mardonius was killed, and Pausanias became the first Spartan leader to defeat the Persians.

Spartan soldiers formed a wall of shields and shot arrows at Persian soldiers, who thought that the Spartans had retreated.

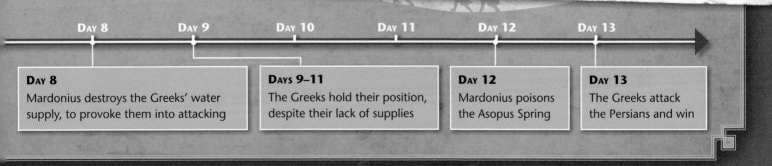

DAY 8

DAY 9

DAY 10

DAY 11

DAY 12

DAY 13

DAY 8
Mardonius destroys the Greeks' water supply, to provoke them into attacking

DAYS 9–11
The Greeks hold their position, despite their lack of supplies

DAY 12
Mardonius poisons the Asopus Spring

DAY 13
The Greeks attack the Persians and win

IN PROFILE: King Xerxes

In Profile

NAME: King Xerxes

TITLE: King of Persia

BORN: 519 BCE

DIED: 465 BCE

King Xerxes was the son of King Darius I of Persia, and he ruled over the Persian Empire from 485 BCE until 465 BCE. Most of what is known about King Xerxes was written by Greek sources, so the information about him often shows him in a bad light.

History tends to judge King Xerxes by his failed attempts to conquer Greece. However, he also expanded the Persian Empire and built many great halls and monuments.

Infamous Moment

King Xerxes is remembered for his decision to invade Greece. Shortly before his death, Xerxes' father, King Darius I, had attempted to invade Greece but failed. King Xerxes planned to invade Greece for the second time. This invasion led to the Persian Wars between the Persian army and the Greek city-states.

King Xerxes and his wife, Queen Esther, were popular with the Persian people.

King Xerxes completed work on the city of Persepolis, the capital of the Persian Empire.

Building Halls and Monuments

King Xerxes oversaw the building of many great halls and monuments, including:

- ❖ the Apadana, an audience hall
- ❖ the Hall of a Hundred Columns, a throne room
- ❖ the Gate of All Nations, also known as the Xerxes gate
- ❖ the Dwelling Place, also known as the Xerxes Palace

He also completed work on the Persian capital of Persepolis, which was begun by his father, King Darius I.

What You Should Know About...

King Xerxes

- ❖ King Xerxes's father seized power over the Persian Empire before Xerxes was born. All Persian kings were supposed to show that they were related to Cyrus the Great, but King Darius was not.

- ❖ Xerxes was Darius's second son. He was given the throne because his mother was believed to be related to Cyrus the Great.

- ❖ Throughout his time as king, Xerxes sought to **legitimize** his rule, because his father was not related to Cyrus the Great.

The Decline of the Spartan Hoplites

Historians believe that the decline of the Spartan hoplites occurred due to reduced numbers of Spartiate citizens, and the Theban defeat of Sparta.

Decrease in Spartiate Citizens

As the number of Spartiate citizens decreased, there were fewer citizens available to fight in the Spartan army. At the beginning of the 500s BCE there were thought to be about ten thousand Spartiate citizens, yet by around 250 BCE there were believed to be fewer than seven hundred citizens. The conservative aristocracy of Sparta was not willing to allow the periokoi to become citizens. As the number of Spartiate citizens decreased, Sparta's land and wealth were held by fewer and fewer families. The gap between rich Spartiate citizens and the periokoi and helots became larger and larger.

Defeat By the Thebans

The Theban defeat of Sparta played a significant role in the decline of the Spartan hoplites. In 371 BCE, the Battle of Leuktra was fought between the Thebans and the Spartan army. The Spartan army was defeated and many of the best Spartan hoplites were killed. The Spartan economy collapsed, and Spartan traditions and ways of living were replaced with those of the Thebans.

The Theban army overthrew Sparta and replaced the Spartan hoplites with Theban soldiers.

Glossary

acclamation   Approving aloud.

Aegean   The body of water and land on which Athens and Sparta were located.

alliance   An agreement between two groups to support each other in times of war.

ambassadors   Representatives from other city-states or empires.

aristocracy   A social class holding titles that are passed down through families.

camaraderie   Friendship and loyalty among a group of people.

casualties   People injured or killed during conflicts.

citizens   Members of a country or a group of people.

city-state   An independent state with its own government, made up of a city and surrounding villages.

conquered   Defeated with force.

deformities   Parts of a person's body that do not function or look in a way considered normal.

democracy   A system of government in which the people vote to elect leaders.

distinctive   Unique and easy to identify.

embody   Represent.

front line   The site where a battle is fought.

initiation   A ceremony or task that a person must perform to join a select group.

lawgiver   A person who makes laws for a society.

legitimize   Make lawful or prove something.

monarchy   A type of government ruled by a single, self-appointed person such as a king.

naval   Fought with navy ships.

offensive   Military attack.

ordained   Ordered or commanded.

outcasts   People who have been rejected from a group of people.

palisade   A fence made of sticks or pointed logs.

phalanx   A group of Greek soldiers who fought together while heavily armed.

public humiliation   Being shamed or disgraced in front of others.

rations   A fixed amount of food and drink.

reeds   Tall grasses that are hollow and flexible.

revolt   Attempt to overthrow the government.

safeguard   A legal protection or guard.

social classes   Groups of people with different degrees of importance.

stealth   A way of moving quietly to avoid being seen.

stipulated   Agreed upon or set out.

superior   Better than.

tyranny   A system of government headed by a person, who uses fear to control others, known as a tyrant.

uprisings   Slaves fighting against the authority of their masters.

war tacticians   People who are skilled at planning military campaigns.

Index